Hymns of the Holy Eastern Church

By Rev. John Brownlie
This Edition Edited by Anthony Uyl

Woodstock, Ontario, Canada 2018

Hymns of the Holy Eastern Church

Hymns of the Holy Eastern Church

With Introductory Chapters on the History, Doctrine, and Worship of the Church

By Rev. John Brownlie

This Edition Edited by Anthony Uyl

The text of Hymns of the Holy Eastern Church is all in the Public Domain. The layout and Devoted Publishing logo are Copyright ©2018 Devoted Publishing. This edition is published by Devoted Publishing a division of 2165467 Ontario Inc.

**What kind of philosophies do you have?
Let us know!**

Visit our website: www.devotedpublishing.com
Contact us at: devotedpub@hotmail.com
Visit us on Facebook: @DevotedPublishing

Published in Woodstock, Ontario, Canada 2018.

For bulk educational rates, please contact us at the above email address.

ISBN: 978-1-77356-249-0

Table of Contents

PREFACE 4
    Footnotes: 5
INTRODUCTION 6
    Footnotes: 10
Hymns of the Holy Eastern Church 23
    ANTIPHON A 23
    ANTIPHON B 24
    ANTIPHON G 25
    TROPARIA 26
    TROPARION FROM THE THIRD CANONICAL HOUR[3] 27
    Footnotes: 27
    KONTAKION-AUTOMELON[4] 28
    Footnotes: 28
    STICHERON IDIOMELON 29
    APOLUTIKION 30
    TROPARIA 31
    TROPARIA 32
    STICHERA OF APOCREOS 33
    STICHERA OF APOCREOS 34
    From the KURIAKE TES TURINEZ . 35
    From the KURIAKE TES TURINES .. 36
    STICHERON 37
    TROPARIA 38
    TROPARIA 39
    TROPARIA 40
    STICHERA 41
    STICHERON OF THE RESURRECTION 42
    STICHERA OF THE RESURRECTION 43
    STICHERA OF THE RESURRECTION 44
    APOLUTIKION of the RESURRECTION 45
    STICHERA ANATOLIKA 46
    STICHERA OF THE ASCENSION ... 48
    HYMN TO THE TRINITY 49
    HYMN TO THE TRINITY 50
    HYMN TO THE TRINITY 51
    ORDER OF HOLY UNCTION 52
    ORDER OF HOLY UNCTION 53
    FROM THE CANON OF THE DEAD 54
    IDIOMELA OF S. JOHN THE MONK 55
    STICHERON 56
    STICHERA 58
    STICHERA 59
Centos and Suggestions 60
    VAIN THE BLISS FROM EARTH THAT SPRINGS 60
    HAIL! THE MORN WITH GLADNESS CROWNED 61
    CLOSE BESIDE THE HEART THAT LOVES ME 62
    THE TIME SHALL SURELY COME 63
    THE TRANSFIGURATION 64
    BEYOND THE CLOUDS OF HEAVEN 65
    TRIPLE BEAM OF GLORY 66
    O GOD OF LIGHT AND LIFE AND JOY 67
    THE MORN IN BEAUTY BREAKS . 69
    SEE WHERE THE ORB OF DAY 70

Rev. John Brownlie

PREFACE

The generous reception given to a former series of renderings of Hymns from the Office Books of the Greek Church [1] by those who are best qualified to judge, and the gratifying fact that already no fewer than five pieces from that series have secured a place in the revised edition of one of our most valued permanent Hymnals, encourage the translator to pursue his work in this department of devotional literature.

No apology is needed for this additional volume on a subject too little known, the contents of which are an earnest attempt to acquaint our people still further with the valuable praise literature of the Eastern Church.

We are still far from realising the unity of the Church of Christ in the world, when that section of it which is historically nearest The Christ--which joins hands with Him and with His Apostles--is practically ignored. Why this should be, let our Christian scholars answer. About a year ago the Rev. R. M. Moorsom, of Winchester, published his Renderings of Church Hymns, containing, among others, twenty translations from the Service Books of the Eastern Church. For that valuable addition to our hymnody, the Christian Church in our land is under a debt of gratitude to Mr. Moorsom; but he and the very few others who have sought to interest the Church in a subject so rich and so attractive, have as yet but touched its fringe.

Of the forty-six pieces in this volume, forty-two appear for the first time in English verse. While leaving critics to pass their verdict on the value of the work, the translator can yet justly claim to have made a substantial addition to our English hymnody from Eastern sources.

The renderings have all been made from the Service Books, the edition used being the one printed at Venice,--with the exception of the Triodion, which belongs to the Athens edition.

To enable any who are interested in the subject, and who may have access to the Service Books, to compare the renderings with the original text, the title of the book, and the number of the page where it can be seen, are given in each case.

The Introductory chapters on the History, Sacraments, and Worship of the Church, are given in the hope that they may be the means of removing prejudices and misconceptions, and of awakening some degree of interest in the Eastern Church.

For much of the information contained in these chapters the translator is indebted, among other works, to Neale's History of the Holy Eastern Church, Stanley's History of the Eastern Church, King's Rites and Ceremonies of the Greek Church, and Gibbon's Decline and Fall of the Roman Empire. But many of the facts were collected a few years ago during a residence in the East.

J. B.
Trinity Manse,

Portpatrick, Nov. 1, 1902.

Rev. John Brownlie

Footnotes:

1. Hymns of the Greek Church. Translated, with Introduction and Notes. Oliphant, Anderson & Ferrier: Edinburgh, 1900.

INTRODUCTION

I

The Eastern Church is little known in the West, and it would seem that there is not much desire on our part to alter that condition of things. As the Eastern Hemisphere is separated from the Western by the Ural and Carpathian ranges, so is Eastern Christendom separated from Western Christendom, and more effectually, by the mountain barriers which our ignorance, prejudice, and indifference have set up. But it is well to remember the German proverb, Behind the mountains are also people, and that the people who are behind those mountains which have been the growth of centuries, form nearly one-fourth of the followers of the Faith of Christ, or about one hundred million souls.

The causes which have led to this indifference on the part of the West towards the East are many, but there are two which might be mentioned as being perhaps the chief.

(I.) The first of these is the inherent peculiarity of temperament, which finds its expression in habits of thought, and modes of action, in the East, against which the spirit of the West frets, and for which it has neither sympathy nor toleration. The quiet, meditative restfulness of the East--its satisfaction with past attainment in the matter of Doctrine and Worship, its wistful retrospective gaze upon magnificent accomplishment, which the experience of centuries of trial has only intensified, are totally alien to the active, speculative, hopeful spirit of the West. Attainment is the boast of the East, and in that it rests content. Progress, achievement, is the craze of the West. Those temperaments, so obviously diverse, have for long parted company.

(II.) The other is the great Roman Church. Inspired with that spirit which commends itself to the Western mind--its activity, its aptitude to fit itself to the ever-changing circumstances of the times, its progressive spirit, its thirst for achievement--characteristics without which it could scarcely have survived amid the crash of falling empire, and the chaos of barbaric anarchy which marked its birth--that Church for the past nine centuries has obtruded itself upon our attention, and claimed, nay demanded, our consideration. It pervades the West, its advocates are ubiquitous, its influence is everywhere felt. It was a knowledge of that Church and a very real acquaintance with its spirit and methods, which enabled the reformers of the sixteenth and seventeenth centuries to successfully wage war with it; and we realise that, in these days, to retain our freedom we must keep ourselves in touch with it, and by full and fresh acquaintance continue armed against its persistent aggressiveness. We are out of touch with the East, at no point do we come in contact with it; we have nothing to fear, though we might have something to hope from it. But we are in the West, and whether we will or not the Roman Church is always with us, and unceasingly demands our attention. So the Eastern Church fades from our view: out of sight it is out of mind, and it is the Roman Church that bars our vision.

Rev. John Brownlie

But the Eastern Church deserves better at our hands than to be thus forgotten. In these days of unrest, when men's minds are unsettled on so many questions, a strange, alluring calm pervades our spirit when we overtop the barriers and look down upon the peace and quiet of Eastern Christendom. There, in all her pristine simplicity and attractiveness, as in the golden days of the Empire, as in the fierce conflict of the early middle ages when John of Damascus whetted the sword for the conflict, so now under the misrule and tyranny of the Turk, she holds in quiet restfulness the simple faith committed to her by the Apostles and Fathers, the same Church now as then.

Do we forget that the Fathers of the Eastern Church formulated our doctrines, and shaped our Creed, guarding it in every item with jealous care? Do we forget that the Churches founded by the apostles in Syria and Asia Minor still hold by the apostolic doctrine, and are parts of that great Church? Do we forget that the creed framed at Nicea is practically our creed, even as it is the creed of the Eastern Church? Do we forget that with unbroken succession, from the dawn of Christianity down to the present day, the bishops of that Church have handed on the torch of truth? We reap the blessings of Eastern fidelity to Christian truth, and forget, or ignore, the source whence it came to us. The high-sounding pretensions of Rome hide the facts of the case from us, and Rome, the first great dissenter from the Catholic Church, would not only claim for herself what does not belong to her, but would brand as schismatic and heretic all who differ from her in doctrine or practice. What modern Christendom would have been, had the Roman schism of 1054 never taken place, it is difficult to conceive. The suggestion opens up to our minds an alluring prospect, for we cannot forget that the revolt of the reformed faith in the sixteenth century was not from the faith of the East, but from the Roman Church with its accumulation of intolerable abuse.

Such thoughts should incline us sympathetically towards the Church of the East, and enable us to overtop the barriers which have been raised by incidents of history and unfounded prejudices and differences of temperament, which in no way affect the fact of our indebtedness to that Church, and consequently her claim upon our intelligent interest.

But we are told that, after all, there is little difference between the Roman Church and the Greek Church--that the abuses of the one are the abuses of the other. That, we shall see shortly, is not the case. And we are told, too, that the Greek Church is a dead Church, and without missionary zeal. How a Church that has stretched out its hands to the farthest east, bestowing the blessings of the Gospel upon Tartar and Indian; southward, planting the Cross in Arabia, Persia, and Egypt; northward, diffusing light to the limits of Siberia, can be termed a non-missionary Church, is difficult to understand. How a Church that has fought hand to hand with idolatry, not only in the early ages when her spirit was young, but also during the past six centuries under the abominable superstition of the Turk, retaining her faith in Christ through it all, can be termed a dead Church, does not readily appear. No Church has provided more martyrs to the Christian Faith; and even during the course of the nineteenth century, in the Lebanon, at Damascus, throughout Syria, and in Armenia, men and women have chosen death rather than abandon their faith in Christ. If under persistent, unceasing persecution--not for generations, but for centuries--a Church can hold to its faith and maintain its testimony, the term dead cannot be applied to it. When in 1453 the Turk entered Constantinople, the history of the

Greek empire was closed, but not that of the Church. She accepted the change of circumstances; and when her temples were despoiled, and her worship profaned, still held to her faith in Christ. If missionary zeal has languished, if life is faint in the midst of such experiences, is it to be wondered at? The struggle with oppression has been long, but now that the Ottoman Empire totters to its fall, the prospect brightens, and the Church which has so nobly maintained the conflict will doubtless reap her reward when the tyranny, which is meanwhile co-extensive with her beneficent sway, has for ever been removed.

Prior to the great schism of 1054, when the See of Rome separated from the East, and the Pope excommunicated Michael Cerularius, Patriarch of Constantinople, in East and West, Christendom was practically one. The causes which led to that separation, which was fraught with momentous and far-reaching issues for Christianity, may be briefly referred to. They had their beginnings in the far past.

The building of Constantinople in A.D. 330 by the Emperor Constantine on the site of the ancient Byzantium, and the subsequent transference of the seat of government to that city, were in reality the prime causes leading to that disagreement and alienation, which grew in intensity and broadened, till they reached the point of entire separation.

Prior to that event, Byzantium was but one of the many Sees of the Eastern Church, but thereafter its rank rose with the rising importance of the city, till at the Council of Constantinople, A.D. 381, which closed the Arian controversy, the bishop of Constantinople was elevated to the second rank after the bishop of Rome, on the ground that Constantinople was the New Rome. No pre-eminence of jurisdiction was granted at that time, but it came in due course when, at the Council of Chalcedon, A.D. 451, the canon of A.D. 381, conferring second rank, was confirmed, and a range of jurisdiction granted. Against all this Rome, of course, protested emphatically, the Pope excommunicating the patriarchs of Constantinople and Alexandria, and for forty years the East and West were practically separated. At the end of that term, however, excommunication was withdrawn on the acknowledgment of the supremacy of Rome; but the estrangement continued and broadened. It was aided, on the one hand by the pride of the Greeks who plumed themselves on their unbroken succession from the Apostolic Church, their use of the language of the Apostles which was little known in the West, their introduction of Christianity into the West, and their formulation of Christian doctrine; and on the other hand, by the old spirit of Rome, which aspired to world-wide dominion both in Church and in State, and could ill brook rivalry on the part of the Greeks. The estrangement found its completion in 1054, when the addition of the word Filioque to the Latin creed, by which the Roman See expressed its belief in the doctrine of the double procession of the Holy Ghost--from the Father and the Son--a doctrine against which the Greek Church had emphatically protested, supplied the ground for a renewal of the quarrel which this time resulted in separation complete and final, Pope Leo IX. excommunicating the patriarch of Constantinople.

The responsibility for the great schism undoubtedly lies with Rome, and that should be remembered for all time. The introduction of Filioque into the Creed was a proceeding by no means called for. Christians could quite well have lived and worked together without dogmatising on that particular; but a pretext had to be found, and Filioque supplied it.

II

Prior to the fall of the Empire in the middle of the fifteenth century, the Greek Church comprised within her borders, Greece, Illyricum (Dalmatia), the islands of the Archipelago; Russia; Asia Minor, Syria, and Palestine; Egypt, Nubia, and Abyssinia; Arabia, Persia, and Mesopotamia. After that disaster she fell into a dependent condition in those territories secured by the Turk. In the eighteenth century Russia claimed separation from Constantinople, and has been governed since by a Holy Synod; and when the new kingdom of Greece was established in the early part of last century, the Church there, in like manner, claimed a distinct organisation. Scattered portions of the Church, chiefly in Hungary, Servia, Bosnia, Bulgaria, and in Poland, which, while following the Greek rite, accepted the supremacy of the Pope, united themselves, A.D. 1590, to the Roman See. But those Uniat Greeks, as they were termed, after 250 years, returned to the Eastern Church, in part associating themselves with the Russian Church, and in part with the See of Constantinople. Servia has now its own Metropolitan.

At the present time, the Eastern Church may be thus grouped--
I. The Greek Church proper.
II. The Heretical Churches.
III. The Russian Church.

I. The Greek Church comprises those peoples who speak the Greek language. Among these are the independent Church of Greece, the Apostolic Churches of Asia Minor, and those Uniats in the northern part of the Balkan Peninsula who returned to their former allegiance to the Patriarch of Constantinople. In this group we may also include the independent Church of Servia.

II. The Heretical Churches are self-supporting Churches in the countries in which they are situated. They are termed heretical on account of their revolt from the jurisdiction of Constantinople. They hold with the rest of the Church to the doctrine of the Nicene creed as drawn up at the first two Councils, but reject the decisions of the subsequent Councils. They are the Churches in Egypt, Syria, and Armenia, and in those countries known as Kurdistan.

The causes which gave rise to those so-called Heretical Churches are not a little interesting, but cannot be gone into here at any length. They may, however, be referred to as shewing the relation of the Churches of the East to the various Councils.

The Heretical Churches of the East owe their existence to the actions of the General Councils subsequent to the Councils of Nicea and Constantinople. At these the doctrines accepted by Orthodox and Heretical Churches alike were distinctly expressed. But when to the decisions of those Councils there came to be added the decrees of succeeding Councils, certain Churches revolted. Those universally accepted doctrines were that Christ was consubstantial with the Father (homoousios), and that He, the Son of God, became man (enanthropesas). It was, however, only when theologians tried to make plain what was meant by the latter phrase, that it prickled with disputable points. The differences of opinion emerging took two types. One of these so thoroughly divided the Divine from the human nature in Christ, as almost to destroy altogether any real union. Another insisted on an absorption of the human in the Divine, such as would disfigure both, and by that absorption create a distinct nature. The former, the separation of the natures, became the doctrine of the Churches of Chaldea, while the latter was adopted by the Churches of Egypt.

The Nestorians in like manner accept the decrees of the first two Councils, and refuse to entertain the additions made by the latter Councils, characterising them as unwarranted alterations of, or additions to the findings of the first two Councils. The Monophysites accept the addition of Chalcedon and of all the Councils following it.

The third General Council, that of Ephesus, decreed that the title Theotokos (God-bearer) should be applied to the Virgin, and at the Council of Chalcedon this was repeated, affirming that Christ was born of the Theotokos, according to the manhood; the same Symbol affirming that two natures are to be acknowledged in Christ, and that they are indivisible and inseparable. Thus it was that the Nestorians repudiated the decrees alike of Ephesus and Chalcedon, by repudiating the term Theotokos and holding the duality of Christ's nature so as to lose sight of the unity of His Person.

There was nothing for it, therefore, but to separate from the Greek Church (orthodox), and in separation from that Church they became most extensive and powerful.

At the Council of Chalcedon, the fourth General Council, the now widely acknowledged doctrine in all the Churches of the West, as also in the Orthodox Greek Church, was declared, that Christ was to be acknowledged in two natures. The Monophysites--those who held by the one nature theory--revolted, and gave rise to many sects, and to three Churches--the Coptic Church of Egypt, the Abyssinian Church, and the Jacobite Church of Syria. [2]

The Armenian Church is in much the same position; but it has been termed even more heretical than the Jacobite, a very erroneous charge against a Church which is really orthodox. The Armenian Church is separated from the Constantinopolitan by the difference which the accidental absence of the Armenian bishop from the Council of Chalcedon made: the decisions of which were never understood, and of course never formally accepted.

III. The Russian Church includes the peoples of that great Empire. Christianity was first preached in Russia at the close of the tenth century, when Prince Vladimir was baptised, A.D. 992. Originally, and for many years this Church, subject to the Patriarch of Constantinople, as already stated, claimed separate jurisdiction in 1721. The Czar is the head of the Church in temporalities, but the Holy governing Synod is the spiritual head, and supplies the place of a patriarch.

Under so many jurisdictions, the Eastern Church is dogmatically one. She has no Confession of Faith; no Thirty-nine Articles: the Bible is her standard, and the Creed of Nicea her expression of dogma.

The Athanasian Creed is found in the Service Books of the Church, but it is not an acknowledged Symbol; and there it differs from the text accepted in the West in the clause relating to the Holy Spirit.

Footnotes:

2. Jacobus Baradaeus, an eminent Syrian theologian, who rejected all decisions of Councils subsequent to Constantinople, 381 A.D.

III

In common with the Roman Church, the Greek Church has seven Sacraments. These are--the Eucharist, Baptism, the Holy Chrism, Penance, Matrimony, Unction of the Sick, and Ordination.

Holy Communion.--In relation to this Sacrament, as indeed to all the Sacraments of the Eastern Church, it is necessary to say that, doctrine being in an altogether undefined state, an outsider has considerable difficulty in realising, in any degree of certainty, what the attitude of mind generally of the Church is, or more exactly ought to be. One cannot help feeling that without the mental subtleness of the East, and the atmosphere and environment of its worship, it is impossible to understand, so as to express it, how this Sacrament is viewed. Eastern theology has not been systematised, and could not be--such subtleties and nice distinctions abound, as would defy systematising.

And nowhere as in this Sacrament do we feel this difficulty more. Transubstantiation as we understand it, and as it is held in the West, is nowhere a doctrine of belief in the Eastern Church, although the language of the service may seem emphatic, and quite unmistakable. Under the operation of the Holy Spirit--not as in the West, after the formula of institution (and this is an important difference) the bread and wine become the precious Body and the precious Blood of our Lord; and when they are partaken of, are as fire and light in us, consuming the substance of sin, and burning the tares of our passions. That all seems plain enough. But what is the nature of this change? In the Western Church the material on the altar--the bread and the wine--are actually changed into the Body and the Blood: they are materially no longer bread and wine: the bread and wine have disappeared, and the Body and Blood of Christ have taken their place. They are, as the term expresses it, transubstantiated.

That is not the view of the Greek Church. The bread and the wine do not change their substance: they are bread and wine, nothing more, to the end, with this difference, it is a subtle one, doubtless, that the Body and Blood of Christ under the operation of the Holy Ghost are there IN that bread and wine. There is, if we might so express it, Insubstantiation. The materials are not changed, but the Body and Blood of Christ are there.

As a rule, persons go to Holy Communion once a year, shortly after confession. The laity communicate in both kinds, and in this particular the Eastern Church differs from the Western, which withholds the cup from the laity. In other particulars the two Churches differ. The wine is mixed twice, not once; the Sacrament is received standing, not kneeling; and the bread is ordinary leavened bread, not unleavened. As noticed in connection with baptism, infants after that Sacrament partake of the cup, and continue to do so till they reach their seventh year. At that age they are expected to go to Confession, and thereafter they communicate in both kinds.

There are three methods of communion practised in the Eastern Church, (1) Giving the bread first, and thereafter the cup, as is the uniform custom in the West. (2) The priest gives the bread, and the deacon gives the wine with a spoon. (3) The bread is broken into crumbs, and put into the wine, and both are given together in a spoon.

Before the people separate, the priest distributes the Antidoron. The bread of the Eucharist is called the Gift, and the portion which is afterwards distributed is for the use of those who have not communicated, and is given in place of the gift. It is carried home, and may be used by the person himself, or given to any who are sick, or who for other reasons were absent from the celebration, and is partaken of fasting. The services both before and after Communion are in many cases exceedingly beautiful.

Baptism.--The Eastern Church observes infant baptism, but insists on trine immersion--in the name of the Father, and of the Son, and of the Holy Ghost. A priest is the celebrant; but in cases of sudden and serious illness any orthodox person may perform the rite. In the event, however, of the sick person recovering, a priest must fill in and complete the office.

The form of the service is briefly as follows. The child having been brought to church, is anointed with oil, which has been blessed for the purpose by the priest, on the breast and back, and on the ears, hands, and feet. Then follows the profession of the faith in which the child is baptized. The water of baptism is thereafter blessed, and the child immersed three times.

The Holy Chrism is the Sacrament of Confirmation in the Eastern Church, and it differs considerably from the Western rite. This Sacrament is given immediately after baptism, not as in the West when the child has come to years of discernment, and in nearly every case by the ordinary priest. Oil is again used, the priest anointing the baptised person with it, making the sign of the Cross--on the forehead, eyes, nostrils, mouth, ears, breast, hands, and feet. Thereafter the child partakes of the wine of the Holy Communion.

Penance.--In the Greek Church Confession has never assumed the objectionable features which so largely characterise that Sacrament in the Roman Church. It is, as far as it can be made such, a means of grace; and when used in a right and proper spirit, helpful to a degree. To quote from a catechism of the Russian Church, "Penance is a mystery, in which he who confesses his sins is, on the outward declaration of the priest, immediately loosed from his sins by Jesus Christ Himself." Or in the language of a former Metropolitan of Moscow--"Confession is a mystery in which sins are forgiven by God, through the means of the priest, to the faithful, when these confess them unreservedly, and believe unhesitatingly in the merits of Christ." At the age of seven every child is expected to come to Confession and to continue coming four times a year ever thereafter.

When the priest has offered up prayer supplicating the mercy of God, the penitent confesses his sins, craving pardon from the just and merciful God, and grace to sin no more. The confessor addressing the penitent reminds him that he has come to God with his sins, and does not confess to man but to God. After he has been dealt with in all faithfulness, the priest tells him that he himself is also an unworthy sinner, and has no power to forgive sins, but relying on the Word of Christ, "Whosesoever sins ye remit," says, "God forgive thee in the world that now is, and in that which is to come."

Penance is prescribed only for mortal sins; for venial sins absolution alone is given, the penitent kneeling while being absolved, although during confession he sat.

Matrimony.--The first duty of the priest towards persons contemplating marriage is to instruct them in the Ten commandments, the Lord's Prayer, and the Creed. Notice of intended marriage is announced in church some weeks prior to the event, and the ceremony is carried out in church before witnesses.

The Office for Matrimony has two parts, one dealing with betrothal, and the other with the marriage. These may be performed at the same time, or separately, as the case may demand.

Taking the betrothal first. After prayer for blessing upon the persons, the priest takes two rings, one of gold and one of silver, and giving the ring of gold to the man says, "A., the servant of God, is betrothed to B., the handmaid of God, in the name of the Father, and of the Son, and of the Holy Ghost, now and ever and to the ages of ages, Amen." Afterwards taking the silver ring, and giving it to the woman, he says, "B., the handmaid of God," etc. The godfather then changes the rings, giving the gold ring to the woman, and the silver ring to the man, an expressive act, proclaiming to the bridegroom that he must learn to accommodate himself to the weakness of the bride, and that she has now become sharer of his goods. Then follows the Coronation, or marriage proper. After words of instruction and prayer, the priest takes the crowns, and first of all crowns the bridegroom, saying, "A., the servant of God, is crowned for B., the handmaid of God, in the name of the Father," etc. Then he crowns the bride, using the same formula. The words are repeated three times in each case, the sign of the Cross being made each time. The crowns are, as a rule, the property of the Church, and according to the wealth or poverty of the people are made of precious metal or of tin. The priest then takes the common cup and gives to the bridegroom first, and then to the bride, to drink. Later, the priest removes the crowns, and after prayer the friends come forward with their congratulations, the bridegroom and the bride kiss each other, and the priest pronounces the dismissal.

Second and third marriages, while allowed, are not looked upon with favour, and the Church shows its disapprobation in several ways. They are not crowned, and the words of the service for such marriages have subtle allusions to their unworthiness. The priest prays, "Give unto them the conversion of the publican, the tears of the harlot, and the confession of the thief, that through repentance they may be deemed worthy of Thy Heavenly Kingdom." The priest does not present Himself at the wedding feast, nor are the parties allowed to partake of the Sacraments of the Church for the space of two years. Fourth marriages are unlawful.

Unction of the Sick.--This Sacrament must not be confounded with the Sacrament of Extreme Unction of the Roman Church. It has its authority in the injunction of the Apostle James--"Is any sick among you? let him call for the elders of the Church; and let them pray over him, anointing him with oil in the name of the Lord." The oil is consecrated for the purpose by seven priests, and the Sacrament is not administered unless several priests, usually three, are present. This rule is founded on the use of the plural number by St. James. If possible, the rite is observed in church, but where that is impossible, in the house. According to the Scriptural direction, the priest anoints the sick with oil, and prays God to forgive him, and to cure the body and the soul. In cases of extreme urgency the Communion is thereafter given to the sick.

Ordination.--This Sacrament, giving as it does a place in the succession with apostolic authority, is most jealously guarded. But before speaking of Ordination, it may be useful in the first place to give some description of the vestments worn in the Greek Church, and with which the clergy are robed according to their rank. The origin of the vestments in use in the Greek Church certainly affords much difficulty. It is more than likely that they present fundamentally the dress of the early Greek of comparatively high social standing in apostolic times, with certain very important modifications and additions.

We can find no trace of vestments of any kind whatsoever in the Apostolic Church. The garments worn by the apostles and their companions in work would be the dress of the ordinary Greek of fairly high social standing. During the first three centuries, in which Christianity suffered so much at the hands of her enemies, we cannot think of much alteration on dress taking place in the case of the ministers of religion--men had something else to think about. But quieter times came, and no doubt the alterations would then be made to which we have referred; and we can fancy that in making those alterations regard would be had to symbolism, and that garments to suggest certain facts and functions would be brought into use. In making those modifications and additions there can be little doubt that the vestments of the Jewish priesthood with their symbolism would be, as far as possible, approximated.

That those vestments in the early centuries were purely what they now are, ecclesiastical vestments, we very much doubt. It is more likely that for some time they constituted what we would term the ordinary everyday clerical dress.

The first vestment, and that which is common to every order, is the Stoicharion, which corresponds to the Alb in use in the West. It is a white tunicle, not now of linen as formerly, but of silk. The Epimanikia, or hand-pieces, were formerly made in the shape of the sleeves of a surplice, but are now considerably contracted. They hang down on each side of the arm, and are drawn close to it by cords which are fastened tightly round the wrist. The significance of the vestment is not apparent. They are said to represent the cords with which Christ was bound before being delivered to Pilate. Formerly, only bishops wore the Epimanikia, but now they are worn by all ranks.

The Orarion, or praying vestment, is peculiar to the deacon. It is identical with the Latin Stole, and is thrown over the left shoulder. Its significance is obscure, but it has been represented as symbolising wings, the ministry of the deacon being angelical. Those three vestments constitute the dress of the deacon. The priest has the Stoicharion and the Epimanikia, but instead of the Orarion the Epitrachelion. This vestment is not unlike the stole, but of a different shape. It is not thrown round the neck hanging down the front in two pieces. The head of the priest passes through a hole of sufficient size, and the vestment hangs in front in one piece. Whether it symbolises the easy yoke of Christ we cannot say. The Zone is the next article of vestment, and is worn to bind the Stoicharion and the Epitrachelion together round the waist.

The Phaenolion.--This word is translated cloke in I. Tim., iv. 13, and as a vestment represents the garment which Paul left at Troas with Carpus. It is the Latin Chasuble, but is now much reduced in dimensions. Those five vestments constitute the dress of a priest. The bishop, in addition to the five just mentioned, with the exception of the Phaenolion, for which is substituted the Saccos which represents the robe in which Christ was mocked, has two other vestments, making seven in all. They are the Omorphiona, or Pall. It is fastened round the neck, and is larger than the Latin Dalmatic; and the Epigonation, which is a small ornament made of brocade, or some such stiff material, and of a diamond shape. It is worn hanging at the right side, and may represent the towel with which Christ girded Himself, or if a sword, may be typical of the victory of the Church over sin. No doubt the latter is the correct interpretation, as the words spoken, when it is assumed, would indicate, "Gird Thy sword on Thy thigh, O Thou most Mighty."

The office of Ordination is exceedingly simple and most expressive, and varies according to the rank of the candidate. The minor orders are those of Reader, Singer, Sub-Deacon, and Deacon. If the candidate be a Reader, he is brought to the bishop, who counsels him regarding his duties, and laying his hand upon his head prays over him, ordaining him to his order. He is then robed in the Stoicharion and a copy of the Epistles is put into his hand. If a Singer, he is robed in like manner, and a copy of the Psalter is put into his hand. The office for a Sub-Deacon is more elaborate, as his rank is higher than that of a Reader or a Singer. He is set apart for the exercise of his functions with prayer and counsel, and is robed with the Stoicharion and Zone. The Order of Deacon is a much more important one in the East than in the West. He has duties in connection with the celebration of the Eucharist, as we have already seen, which he alone can perform. He is vested, in addition to the Stoicharion and Zone, with the Orarion, or Stole, which he wears over his left shoulder.

The higher orders begin with the priest. In his case the Orarion is exchanged for the Epitrachelion, and the service is arranged to suit the peculiar functions of his order. The additional higher orders are--Proto-presbyter, Abbot, Archimandrite, Bishop, and Metropolitan or Patriarch. It should be stated that the lower grades are necessary steps to the higher ones, and are, as a rule, permanent.

Unlike the Roman Church, which demands the celibacy of the clergy, the Eastern Church requires of all orders of her parochial clergy that they should be married prior to ordination. Bishops, who, as a rule, are chosen from the monasteries, and are consequently celibates, continue in that state, although a married bishop has not been unknown in the Eastern Church. The practice is founded on the words of St. Paul to Timothy, "A Bishop must be ... the husband of one wife," which they take literally, in a sense which we do not attach to them. Before, therefore, orders can be conferred, the candidate must be married, and if during his incumbency his wife should die, he must give up his parochial duties and retire to a monastery. He cannot put himself right with this requirement of Church discipline by marrying again, for "A bishop must be ... the husband of one wife." If, as we are bound to infer from that prohibition, he is deemed the husband of one wife even after his wife is dead, it is difficult to understand on what principle he is obliged to abandon his duties, seeing that he has fulfilled the apostolic requirement. Such is the practice of the Church: he must be married once, and his wife must be alive during the whole term of his incumbency. We must however bear in mind the objection which the Eastern Church has to second marriages generally, which, while not prohibited, are stigmatised; and perhaps in this objection is to be found the explanation of the general rule.

One other rank should be mentioned--that of Deaconess or Abbess. It ranks above that of Deacon, and was instituted in order to bring conventual establishments, over which they are set, directly under Episcopal jurisdiction.

The minor rites, canons, and offices, and special prayers of the Eastern Church, are too numerous to be dealt with here. Suffice it to say, that there is no event of ecclesiastical importance which has not its appropriate rite, and scarcely an experience of life for which some provision has not been made in the magnificent services of the Church.

One office of universal interest, however, we must refer to shortly, viz., that for Burial. There are five Burial offices in the Euchologion--for a monk, for a priest, for a child, and for laymen (two). It may serve our purpose to take the last as a specimen.

The office begins with the following instruction:--"On the death of one of the orthodox, straightway the relatives send for the priest, who, when he is come to the house in which the remains lie, assumes the Epitrachelion, and burning incense gives the blessing, and the relatives, as is usual, say the Trisagion, the Most Holy Trinity, and the Lord's Prayer." After certain troparia are sung, and prayer offered, the remains are carried to the church and placed in the narthex (page 52). The service, which is long and varied, and most impressive, is made up of scriptural lessons--Psalm i.; The Beatitudes; John v. 24; I. Thess. iv. 13-17; prayers; The Canon of the Dead, which contains eight odes written by Theophanes (eighth century), and the idiomela of John the Monk--presumably John of Damascus--eight in number, the first of which is given in this volume. Towards the close of the service, the priest bows down and kisses the corpse, in which act he is followed by the relatives and friends present. Then the stichera of the last kiss, said to have been written by John of Damascus, are sung, followed by the idiomela. After the priest has given the prayer of absolution, the body is carried to the grave followed by the mourners, the clergy going before chanting the Trisagion. When the remains have been laid in the grave, the priest takes some earth on a shovel, and scatters it crosswise on the body, saying, "The earth is the Lord's and the fulness thereof, the world and they that dwell therein." After the corpse oil has been poured upon the remains the grave is covered, while certain troparia are sung. This office in certain parts is very striking. The stichera of the last kiss, of which a rendering can be seen in Neale's [37]Hymns of the Eastern Church, and the idiomela, which follow, being specially noteworthy.

It is deserving of note that the Eastern Church has a special office for the burial of little children--an appreciation of the honour conferred upon them by Christ in His kingdom, and an acknowledgment of the importance of the child-like spirit, as constituting an essential qualification on the part of those who would enter that kingdom, very beautiful indeed. A rendering of certain stichera from this office is included in this volume.

IV

The following is a typical plan, roughly drawn, of a Greek church.
Typical plan of a Greek Church
1. The Bema; 2. The Altar; 3. The Prothesis; 4. The Diaconicon; 5. The Iconostasis; 6. Doors; 7. The Ambon; 8. The Nave; 9. The Narthex.

From this plan it will be seen at a glance that a Greek Church consists of four parts: (1) The Bema or Sanctuary, which contains the altar, and on either side the Prothesis and the Diaconicon. From the choir the Sanctuary is separated by the Iconostasis, which answers to the altar rails in a Roman Church. (2) In front of the Iconostasis is the Choir, not architecturally separated from the Nave, but occupying the eastern end of it. (3) The Nave. (4) The Narthex. In some of the larger churches there are two Nartheces--the esonarthex and the exonarthex, the latter serving the purpose of an extended porch.

Rev. John Brownlie

To look at the arrangement and detail of the church more particularly--

The (hagion bema) Bema or Sanctuary, for the due celebration of the Holy Mysteries, occupies the eastern end of the church. Only priests are allowed to enter the Bema, and by them it can be entered only after fasting and prayer. The altar which stands in the Bema is built of stone, Christ being the Head of the Corner, and the Foundation Stone, and is furnished with candles, a copy of the Scriptures, and the Cross.

The Prothesis, to the north of the Bema, is a small chapel, on the table of which the sacred offerings are prepared for the altar. The chapel of the Prothesis is separated from the Bema by a wall to which entrance is had by a screened doorway.

The Diaconicon is to the south of the Bema, and contains the sacred utensils and vestments. It is of inferior sanctity, but the clergy of the lower orders are not allowed to enter it.

The Iconostasis is the screen which separates the sanctuary from the choir, and is so called for the reason that certain icons or pictures are depicted on it. It is of panelled wood, sufficiently high to hide the interior of the sanctuary from the worshippers. In some cases it is simply a curtain of some cloth fabric. It has three doors leading to the Prothesis, to the Bema, and to the Diaconicon. On either side of the door giving entrance to the Bema are the icons of our Lord and of the Virgin Mother--the one to the right and the other to the left. Other icons are displayed over the screen, which in many cases is quite a work of art.

In front of the Iconostasis is the choir, and opposite the Holy door leading to the Bema is the Ambon, from which the reader recites the scriptures, and from which, on special occasions, sermons are delivered.

The Nave is that part of the church designed for the accommodation of the male portion of the congregation.

The Narthex gives accommodation to catechumens and penitents, where the Gospels can be heard, but from which the celebration of the Mysteries cannot be witnessed. Late comers usually content themselves with a place in the Narthex in order not to disturb the service. The Narthex is in some cases vaulted, as are also the aisles, so called, over which are galleries for the accommodation of the female portion of the congregation; where these are awanting, women are accommodated in the Narthex, as the division of the sexes during worship is rigidly maintained.

There are no seats in a Greek Church, as the recognised posture during worship is standing. In some churches narrow stalls are built in which the worshipper can stand, leaning forward, and resting his elbows during the long service; and in a church which the writer visited some years ago in Constantinople, there were in those stalls narrow ledges upon which the knee can be rested. Organs are not used in the services; but as the greater part of the service is chanted by the singers, vocal music in some cases is carried to great perfection.

V

The services of the Church are contained in seventeen quarto volumes of closely printed matter. Of these, from a Western point of view, the most important would seem to be:

The Euchologion, which contains the offices of S. Chrysostom and S. Basil, and those for Baptism, Burial, etc.

The Triodion and Pentecostarion contain the services for Lent and the three Sundays preceding it, and for Pentecost. Those two volumes contain the most attractive of all the services of the Church, and their hymnody, which includes much of the work of S. John of Damascus, is incomparable in the whole range of the service books.

The Horologion contains the offices for the eight canonical hours.

The Parakletike or Greater Octoechus, containing the ferial office, is also very rich in hymnody.

The Menaea, of which there are twelve volumes, one for each month of the year, contain the services for saints' days. Service books so many and so voluminous, obviously cannot be in the hands of the people, but it is remarkable to what extent their bulk and intricacies are mastered.

VI

The veneration of saints and relics took its rise on the overthrow of paganism at the time of Constantine. It was very natural that those who had suffered martyrdom at the hands of pagan persecutors should at that time be remembered; and so it came to pass that churches were considered honoured above all others which contained the relics of those martyrs. The bones of Christ's witnesses were removed from their lonely graves, where they had lain long neglected, and were deposited under Christian altars. Saint's days were appointed upon which their deeds were rehearsed and their lives commemorated. From a veneration of the saints it was a short step to their invocation, and what helped the Church to take that step was the difficulty felt by men in regarding Jesus Christ as being at once God, and the Mediator between God and man.

The chief of saints is the Mother of our Lord after the flesh. The title applied to her--Mother of God--is quite intelligible, when we recollect the strife of the Arian controversy, and the determination of the Church to maintain the eternity of the Son and His equality with God.

Saint worship is not countenanced: saints are venerated and invoked, but not worshipped. Ignorant people in the East, even as is the case with ignorant and superstitious people in the West, in all Churches, fall into divers errors; but the invocation of the saints is quite intelligible to the ordinarily instructed minds in the Church, and in their view in no way robs the Three One God of the worship and glory that are due to Him alone.

There are no images in Eastern churches. The onslaught of the iconoclasts of the ninth century stripped Eastern worship of much that beautified and embellished it, but icons, or sacred pictures remained, and are held in as profound veneration, as is the image of any saint in the Church of the West. The icons are very varied in their representations. They represent our Lord and Joseph and Mary; the apostles, saints, and martyrs; and some of them depict interesting incidents from the scriptures. Prayers are said before them, that a devotional spirit may be aroused and sustained by the scene depicted. In the commoner churches those icons are in many cases miserable daubs, but in some of the larger and wealthier churches, and in many of the older buildings where they are executed in mosaic, they are often works of the highest art.

Rev. John Brownlie

Unlike the Roman Church, the Greek Church claims no infallibility. Works of supererogation are not allowed, and there are consequently no grants of indulgence or dispensations. The state of the dead is final--the souls of the departed passing at once into a state of bliss or torment. Purgatory therefore is disallowed, and prayers for the dead are but a pious custom, by which the memory of the departed is kept fresh.

VII

From all this, and from what went before, it must be very obvious to everyone that more than the Filioque contention separates the Greek from the Roman Church. They are diverse in spirit and totally irreconcilable in doctrine and practice. They are in reality two Churches--have been so from the first, and must to all appearance continue so to the end. Nor are we very hopeful that more than a very sympathetic interest in the great apostolic Church can ever result from an increased knowledge of that Church on the part of the Reformed communions of the West--and surely that may be attained; but we must look beyond the self-assertive Roman Church, and by earnest enquiry seek to acquaint ourselves with its history, doctrine, and practice. Such a study will reward us by creating a lasting bond of sympathy with that Church, and by broadening our outlook, which has in the past been too much confined within the limits of the horizon bounding our own communion--a narrowing and pride engendering condition in truth. And from the varied contents of the voluminous service books of the Greek Church--the work of devoted men in the early centuries, who lived so near to the source of our common Christianity--may be culled many flowers with which to beautify the temple of God in these latter days. A specimen of what those books contain may be seen in the contents of this volume.

VIII

It is a very remarkable fact, and certainly not to our credit, that, with the exception of a very few who have made the study a specialty, our educated men shew a most unaccountable ignorance of the most attractive and valuable material for praise and prayer contained in the service books of the Greek Church. We have learning far more than enough, and zeal enough for the pursuit of study in other departments, but this unworked field lies fallow, and no one thinks it worth his while to cultivate it. That the study will reward the student, although not in a material sense--for the meaningless prejudice of the great mass of our people for what is local, and against the thought of the stranger, no matter how beautiful it may be, has still to be reckoned with--yet in the highest sense as conferring upon him a new delight, there can be no doubt; for after the necessary expenditure of patient application, and the passing of the initiatory stages, which in every department of study are somewhat trying, the attraction will begin, and the subject become positively fascinating. To any one having the lyrical gift, and the necessary qualifications for the study of Greek, those service books might prove a mine of treasure inexhaustible. In the seventeen quarto volumes which contain the Greek Offices, there must be material of one kind or another for many thousands of hymns; yet when hymnal compilers ask for hymns from the Greek for their collections, they are not to be had save in the few renderings made by [38]Dr. Neale.

We have not treated the Latin Church after that fashion. There is not a hymn of real merit in the Latin which has not been translated, and in not a few cases oftener than once, with the result that the gems of Latin hymnody are the valued possession of the Christian Church in all English-speaking lands.

One does not proceed far without making some discoveries which may account, to a certain extent, for the neglect of Greek hymnody by those men who are best qualified to pursue the study of it. The writers are not poets in the true sense, and their language is not Greek as we have known it. None of the hymn writers in the service books, or out of them, is a poet of more than ordinary merit; although when John of Damascus forgets his adversaries, and dispenses with his rhythmical peculiarities, and gives forth the utterance of his deep devotional nature, he proves himself to be worthy of the title--The greatest of Greek Christian Poets.

The Greek language lived long and died slowly, and the Christian hymn writers wrote in its decadence. It was then an instrument that had lost its fineness and keenness and polish, not the language of the men whose thoughts still charm the world, and who, by its deft use, gained for themselves and for their work immortality. It has little of the subtlety and suggestiveness of expression, the variety of cadence, and the intellectual possibility of the Greek of the classical writers. It was a language, moreover, crippled by the introduction of ecclesiastical and theological terms and phrases, which stubbornly refuse to lend themselves to classical rhythm. Such a language cannot be expected to have attraction for men to whom the classical poets are a delight.

But it may be objected that Latin hymnody was also produced when the language was in a state of decadence. That is doubtless a statement of fact. But here again we are brought face to face with the dominant influence and age-long sovereignty of the Roman Church in the West, and with the fact that we have derived very largely from her, and to a much less appreciable extent from the Eastern Church. The Roman Church, with all that she had to give, laid hold of the West, and the Eastern Church, lying beyond the mountains, was forgotten.

The hymns of the Greek Church are still in rhythmical prose--strangely oriental in structure--with the exception of those by John of Damascus, which are in iambics; and difficulties confront one on every page. What lines will reward the work of rendering? Prayer, Gospel, psalm, hymn, and exhortation follow each other, and are sometimes strangely interlaced. Where does one begin and another end? Then there is meaningless repetition which must be passed over, and expressions demanding modification. The symbolism is extravagant, and sometimes a single hymn is crowded with figures the most grotesque. Sifting and pruning are needed before a cento can be formed which would commend itself to modern taste.

But when all has been said, there remains much that is both beautiful and attractive. Some of the hymns and fragments are most chaste and tender in their simple expression of Gospel truths, which are so attractive to all true hearts, no matter by what creed dominated.

The remarkable simplicity characterising those hymns, constitutes, strangely it may seem, no small difficulty for the translator. The mere rendering

Rev. John Brownlie

of them into English prose is a comparatively easy task, and can be of no value to any one but the specialist; but to take the unmeasured lines and cut them to form stanzas, and in the process sacrifice nothing of their spirit to the exigencies of rhyme and rhythm, is a task by no means easy. But such drawbacks and difficulties are by no means insurmountable, and with the growing interest in hymnody which characterises our time, it will be strange if, in the years to come, the Greek service books are not made to yield their tribute to the praise of the Christian Church in the West.

The hymns of the service books have a variety of characteristics, and are distinguished by terms, the meaning of which in some cases being extremely vague, and in others to be derived from the subject of the hymn, or from its form, or perhaps from the time, place, or manner in which it is sung. As we have no corresponding words in our language for the greater number of these, it is necessary to retain the original terms.

The Canon is the most elaborate form into which the praise of the Church is cast. A canon consists nominally of nine odes, for the reason that there are nine scriptural canticles employed at Lauds, viz.--(1) The Song of Moses after crossing the Red Sea; (2) The Song of Moses in Deut. xxxii.; The Songs of (3) Hannah; (4) Habakkuk; (5) Isaiah; (6) Jonah; (7) The Three Children, first part, and (8) second part; (9) Mary (the Magnificat), Simeon (Nunc dimittis). But the second ode is generally omitted from the canon on account of the denunciations of God against Israel which it contains, and the canons of the great fast are made up of those rejected odes. As reference is made in each ode to the canticle of the same number--e.g., in the sixth ode to Jonah's prayer in the whale's belly, a considerable amount of ingenuity has been expended to secure that reference. The effect in many cases is somewhat grotesque, but it is remarkable with what skill it has, in so many cases, been accomplished. The result has been to multiply types to an extraordinary extent.

The Hirmos is the first stanza of the ode. It may, or may not, have a connection with the stanzas following, but its function is to give them their rhythmical model.

The Troparion.--Troparia are the stanzas which follow the hirmos. There are usually three in a Greek ode, but the number may exceed that. The term is no doubt derived from the verb trepo, to turn. The troparia turn to the strophes of the hirmos as to a model.

Scattered over the canon is a variety of verses variously named. The Kathisma occurs after the third or sixth ode of the canon. The term is applied to the verse for the reason that it may be sung during a pause in the service, as the word (kathizo) from which the term is derived would indicate.

The Kontakion occurs after the sixth ode. The term may be traced to canticum, or more likely kontos short, but it is of very doubtful derivation.

The Hypacöe, another obscure term, occurs after the third ode.

The Icos follows the kontakion after the sixth ode.

Each ode is followed by a Theotokion (theotokos), God-bearing. This is a troparion dedicated to the Virgin Mother. In some cases a stanza depicting her at the Cross follows, called Staurotheotokion.

Stichera are a series of verses, in some cases taken from the Psalter.

Idiomelon.--Unlike the troparion, which follows the model set by the hirmós, the idiomelon has no model. Stichera Idiomela are a collection of irregular verses.

Kontakion Automelon, is a hymn modelled on any of the set forms.

Exaposteilarion is a verse sung between certain psalms. It may have taken the place of a more ancient form of verse in which God is prayed to send forth His light (Lucerns), or the term may indicate the rule that the exaposteilarion is sung by one of the clergy who is sent (exaposteilon), from his place among the choir, down to the middle of the church, for that purpose.

Apolutikion, is the prayer preceding the close of the office.

One prime characteristic of Greek hymnody should be referred to. Unlike our English hymn which is intensely subjective--in many cases unhealthily so, the Greek hymn is in most cases objective. God, in the glory of His majesty, and clothed with His attributes, is held up to the worship and adoration of His people. Christ in His person and work is set before the mind in a most realistic manner. His birth and its accompaniments; His life; the words He spoke and the works He did; His passion in all the agony of its detail; the denial of Peter; the remorse of Judas; the Crucifixion; the darkness, the terror, the opened graves; the penitent thief, the loud cry, the death;--all are depicted in plain unmistakeable language. So we have in the hymns of the Greek Church a pictorial representation of the history of Redemption which, by engaging the mind, appeals ultimately to the heart and its emotions. Our self-regarding praise is perhaps inevitable, as being the product of the meditative spirit which has its birth and lives in the land of the twilight; but the advantages of the objectiveness of Greek hymnody are so patent, that its cultivation might be fostered by our hymn writers, with advantage to the devotional feeling of our people, and to the worship of the Church.

Hymns of the Holy Eastern Church

ANTIPHON A
(From the Office of Dawn)
en to thlibesthai me, eisakouson mou ton odunon
Parakletike, p. 5
tr., John Brownlie

I

In mine affliction, Lord,
My cry went up to Thee,
And to my sorrowing heart,
Thou gav'st Thy mercy free.

II

When life is parched and dry,
Refreshing streams appear,
And earth's vain sounds are dead
To my enchanted ear.

III

To Holy Ghost be praise,
To Father and to Son:
Almighty Trinity,
While endless ages run.

ANTIPHON B
(From the Office of Dawn)
eis ta ore psuche arthomen
Parakletike, p. 189
tr., John Brownlie

I

Now let our souls ascend
The everlasting hills,
For thence the help of God
Comes to our heartfelt ills.

II

O Christ, with Thy right hand
Thou shalt sustain my soul;
And 'mong deceitful men
My wayward heart control.

III

From Thee renewal comes,
O Holy Ghost Divine;
With Father and with Son,
Co-equal power is Thine.

ANTIPHON G
(From the Office of Dawn)
epi tois eirekosi moi·
Parakletike, p. 189
tr., John Brownlie

I

When came the call to me,
"To God's own house repair,"
Then I was filled with joy,
And sent to heaven my prayer.

II

Within the house of God
Are fearful wonders wrought;--
There a devouring flame
Burns every shameful thought.

III

Thou Spirit, Source of life,
To Thee all praise we give--
To Father and to Son,
In Whom all creatures live.

TROPARIA
exegerthentes tou hupnou, prospiptomen soi
Horologion, p. 2
tr., John Brownlie

I
From the calm of sleep awaking,
Fall we now before Thy feet,
And with angel hymns adoring,
God Almighty we would greet.
Holy, Holy, Holy Thou,
With Thy mercy bless us now.

II
From the couch of rest uprising,
In my soul with brightness shine,
Open Thou my lips to praise Thee,
Blessed Trinity Divine--
Holy, Holy, Holy Thou,
With Thy mercy bless us now.

III
When the Judge shall come for Judgment,
And our deeds are brought to light,
Fearful we shall lift our voices
In the middle of the night--
Holy, Holy, Holy Thou,
With Thy mercy bless us now.

Rev. John Brownlie

TROPARION FROM THE THIRD CANONICAL HOUR[3]

tacheian kai statheran didou paramuthian tois doulois sou, Iesou
Horologion, p. 86
tr., John Brownlie

I

O Jesus, when our spirits mourn,
And heavenly calm would find,
Come to Thy servants in their grief,
And prove that Thou art kind.

II

Stand not afar off from our souls,
Nor from our need depart;
Come with the comfort of Thy love,
And cheer the joyless heart.

III

Thou didst not leave Thy saints of old,
Nor shun their earnest cry;
O ever-present pitying Lord,
Draw nigh to us, draw nigh;

IV

And bind us to Thyself, we pray,
Whose spirits pine for Thee,
That we may hymn Thy glorious name
To all eternity.

Footnotes:

3. Another rendering of this Troparion may be found at page 57 of Hymns of the Greek Church, by the present translator.

KONTAKION-AUTOMELON[4]
psuche mou! psuche mou! anasta, ti katheudeis;
Horologion, p. 369
tr., John Brownlie

I

Wake, my soul! In careless slumber,
Wherefore wilt Thou longer lie?
Wake! for lo, the end approacheth,
And the Judgment draweth nigh.

II

Christ our Lord is ever present,
Sober therefore wait His call,
That the lovingkindness spare thee
Of the Lord who filleth all.

Footnotes:

4. A rendering of this Kontakion will be found in Mr. Moorsom's volume, page 11.

STICHERON IDIOMELON
(Hymn of Anatolius)
he basileia sou, Christe ho Theos
Menaion, December 25, p. 192
tr., John Brownlie

I

Firm through the endless years,
Thy kingdom stands secure,
And Thy dominion evermore,
Through ages shall endure.

II

Thou from the Holy Ghost,
Incarnate cam'st to earth,
And, Christ our God! didst stoop
To share man's lowly birth.

III

Thou cam'st on us to shine,
Light from Eternal Light!
And now the Father's brightness rests
On those who dwelt in night.

IV

O, everything that breathes,
To Thee gives homage now--
The glory of Almighty God,
The Father's image, Thou.

V

O Thou Who shinest forth,
Incarnate God most High,
Who art, and wast in ages gone,
To us bring mercy nigh.

APOLUTIKION
he gennesis sou Christe ho Theos hemon
Horologion, p. 252
tr., John Brownlie

I

Thy Birth upon our world hath given,
O Christ, the truth from highest heaven;
And they who served the stars of night,
Are taught to own a truer Light.
Led by the stars' ethereal sheen,
The Sun of Righteousness is seen;
And night that in their bosom dwells,
The Dayspring from on high dispels.

Rev. John Brownlie

TROPARIA

(From the Canon for Apocreos)
Ode I
hote hexeis ho Theos en muriasi kai chiliasi
Triodion, p. 24
tr., John Brownlie

I

When with Powers of heaven attending,
Angel hosts ten thousand strong,
Christ the Lord to earth descending,
Brings the hour expected long;
Rising to the clouds in air,
Give us grace to meet Thee there.

II

When for Judgment, earth awaiting
Looks towards the awful throne,
Word nor deed of mine relating,
Ne'er my penitence disown;
From the ill in life I've done,
Save me, Thou Almighty One.

TROPARIA
(From the Canon for Apocreos)
Ode III
ho kurios erchetai
Triodion, p. 20
tr., John Brownlie

I

When Christ the Lord shall come,
Who unashamed shall greet Him?
Be ready, thou my soul,
And go thou forth to meet Him.

II

When anger clouds Thy face,
How shall I then adore Thee?
In mercy spare me Lord,
When bowed with grief before Thee.

III

To Thee my cry ascends,
O God, in mercy save me;
And when Thy judgment comes,
Let not my sins enslave me.

STICHERA OF APOCREOS
echesousi salpinges
Triodion, p. 22
tr., John Brownlie

I

When the trumpet's sound shall wake
All the tenants of the tomb,
Men with terror then shall quake,
But the righteous hopeful rise
To secure the promised prize.

II

Severed from the just that day,
Sinners crying in their woe
Pass to chastisement for aye,
Trembling 'neath the awful rod,
Of the stern decree of God.

III

Lord of glory, by Thy grace
Come in pity to our aid;
Make us worthy of a place
With the just who dwell with Thee
In Thy bliss, eternally.

STICHERA OF APOCREOS
bibloi anoigesontai
Triodion, p. 22

I

Surely comes the dreadful day
When before the judgment bar
Men shall stand in vast array,
And the books of God reveal
Deeds of life that men conceal.

II

At the gnashing and the tears,
Every heart shall melt with grief,
While the sinner filled with fears
By the doom of judgment goes
To a life of endless woes.

III

Wherefore we entreat thee, Lord,--
Thou Who art exceeding good,--
Spare us, who with one accord,
Hymn the grace divinely broad
Of our ever-pitying God.

Rev. John Brownlie

From the KURIAKE TES TURINEZ
Or the Sunday upon which cheese is eaten immediately preceding the Monday before Lent
Ode I
deuro psuche mou athlia
Triodion, p. 63

I

Mourn, O my soul, thy primal sin,
As memory brings the past to mind,
When, robbed of innocence, the joys
Of Paradise were left behind.

II

For of Thy lovingkindness great,
Thou, who didst earth and all things frame,
Mad'st from the clay Thy creature man,
With angels to adore Thy name.

III

And through the riches of Thy grace,
O Lord and Maker, Thou didst plant
Fair paradise where I might share
Its richest fruits nor suffer want.

IV

Ah! woe is me, my wretched soul,
God gave its fadeless fruits to thee;
Why didst thou then His law transgress,
And eat from that forbidden tree?

From the KURIAKE TES TURINES
Ode VII
ho despozon ton aionon panton kurios
Triodion, p. 66

I

Eternal Ruler, Thou didst will
To give me form and grace divine;
But lured to sin by serpent skill,
I have provoked that wrath of Thine.
In anger cast me not away,
But call me back, O God, I pray.

II

Ah! woe is me, a robe of shame
Hides what my stole of light adorned;
Hear me, I call upon Thy name,
My Saviour, let me not be scorned;
In anger cast me not away,
But call me back, O God, I pray.

III

O, I was wounded in the soul,
And exiled from the joys I knew;
My Saviour, Thou canst make me whole,
And Thou art pitiful and true.
In anger cast me not away,
But call me back, O God, I pray,

Rev. John Brownlie

STICHERON
From the KURIAKE TES TURINES
ta plethe ton pepagmenon moi deinon
Triodion, p. 63

Ah! woe is me because of sin,
I tremble as I look within
And view my guilty state;
But like Thy servant in Thy word,
I cry, "Have mercy on me, Lord,"
Because Thy mercy's great.

TROPARIA
(From the Canon of the Resurrection)
Ode IV
tis hautos Soter, ho ex Hedom
Parakletike, p. 7

I

What Saviour comes from Edom,
With garments dyed in red?
Who is it wears the thorn crown
Upon His wounded head?
Who is it dies to set us free?
The Holy One of Israel He.
Glory we give with one accord
To Thy blest Resurrection, Lord.

II

O people disobedient,
With shame your Saviour see;
For, He you called to judgment,
And nailed upon the tree,
Hath burst the bands that would enslave,
And risen a victor from the grave.
Glory we give with one accord,
To Thy blest Resurrection, Lord.

Rev. John Brownlie

TROPARIA

(From the Canon of the Resurrection)
Ode VII
ephrixe ge, apestraphe helios
Parakletike, p. 9

I

Then the earth in terror shook,
And the sun grew dark in wonder;
Then the Temple veil was torn,
And the rocks were rent asunder;--
For the Just One, God most glorious,
Died upon the Cross victorious.

II

O Most High, Whom heaven adores,
Thou wast born to us in weakness,
Bore the scourging and the wounds,
Died upon the Cross in meekness;--
Now o'er death we rise victorious,
By the power of God most glorious.

TROPARIA
(From the Canon of the Resurrection)
Ode VIII
ho boulesei hapanta poion
Parakletike, p. 9

I

Word of God, Who by Thy will
Madest all things as we see them;
By Thy glorious Passion, Thou,
From the shade of death didst free them.

II

We would join the glad refrain,
Ceaseless sung by all creation,
To the praise of Him whose works
Wake our souls to adoration.

III

Shattered now the bars of death,
Hades' gates are burst asunder,
For the Word of life arose
While creation gazed in wonder.

IV

To Thy Name eternal praise
Every heart and voice engages;
All Thy works exalt Thy Name,
Through the endless course of ages.

Rev. John Brownlie

STICHERA

(Sung after the Canon for Easter Day)
humnoumen sou Christe, to soterion pathos
Pentecostarion, p. 5

I

Thy glorious rising on the first of days,
We come adoring, and with grateful praise
Thy saving Passion sing in joyful lays;--
With trumpet sound His praise advance.

II

O Christ Who, on the Cross in dark dismay
Didst vanquish death and cast his bands away,--
Almighty, in our life give peace, we pray;
Praise Him with cymbals in the dance.

III

Thou Christ Who, from the depths of hades brought
The life to mortal man his spirit sought;
May we with pure heart hymn Thee as we ought;--
With trumpet sound His praise advance.

IV

We praise Thee that in condescension Thou,
Of Virgin born, to man's estate didst bow,
One with th' Eternal Father then as now;--
Praise Him with cymbals in the dance.

V

He, on the Cross Who freely bare our woes,
And from the grave a glorious Victor rose,
Now on the world His saving grace bestows;--
With trumpet sound His praise advance,
Praise Him with cymbals in the dance.

STICHERON OF THE RESURRECTION
anastaseos hemera, kai lamprunthomen te panegurei
Pentecostarion, p. 5

I

The Day of Resurrection!
Let gladness light each face;
And in our solemn concourse give
To each a kind embrace;
For Christ the Lord hath risen,
And death by death is slain;
The silent dwellers in the tomb
Are called to life again.

II

To those who love or hate us,
"Our brethren," let us say;
Be all with joy forgiven,
This Resurrection Day.
For Christ the Lord hath risen,
And death by death is slain,
The silent dwellers in the tomb
Are called to life again.

Rev. John Brownlie

STICHERA OF THE RESURRECTION
kurie, esphragismenou tou taphou
Parakletike, p. 193

I

When wicked hands had firmly sealed
The silent tomb,
Then cam'st Thou forth, O Christ, as from
The Virgin's womb.

II

Thine Incarnation angels viewed
With wondering gaze;
And soldiers saw the empty tomb
In strange amaze.

III

Search they in vain, those mysteries lay
In night concealed:
The God-man and His rising were
For ever sealed.

IV

Yet to the humble who by faith
Their Lord adore,
Those mysteries fade before their sight
For evermore.

V

Grant us who sing those mysteries now
A claim to praise;
And let Thy mercy bless our lives,
Now, and always.

STICHERA OF THE RESURRECTION
to pathei sou, Christe, pathon eleutherothemen
Parakletike, p. 2

I

Wherefore on the Cross uplifted,
Bore the Lord our anguish sore?
That He might from suffering save us,
By those wounds for evermore.

II

Wherefore from the grave triumphant,
Came our Lord that radiant day?
That the bondage of corruption
Might for ever yield its sway.

III

Let the heavens resound with gladness,
Praises ring through all the earth;
Let the nations all before him,
Clap their hands with joyous mirth.

IV

To the Cross that bore our Saviour
Were our sins in mercy bound;
By the death of Him Who loved us,
Life for all mankind is found.

V

Glory unto God the Father,
Glory unto Christ the Son,
Glory to the Holy Spirit,
Now, and while the ages run.

Rev. John Brownlie

APOLUTIKION of the RESURRECTION
tou lithou sphragisthentos hupo ton Ioudaion
Parakletike, p. 3

I

O come and let us worship Christ,--
Ye people bow before Him,
Who from the dead a Victor rose,--
Sing praises and adore Him.
'Alleluia.

II

The stone was sealed upon the tomb,
And soldiers guard were keeping,
Where in the cold embrace of death
The Christ of God was sleeping.
'Alleluia.

III

Shone in the east the morning star,
The hills with light were glowing,
The Christ arose, upon the world
His light and life bestowing.
'Alleluia.

IV

Wherefore from highest heaven the powers--
Their songs of victory blending,--
Give glory to our Mighty Lord,
And to His reign unending.
'Alleluia.

STICHERA ANATOLIKA
hesperinen proskunesin
Pentecostarion, p. 14

I

Thee, as the evening light declines,
O Christ, unfading light, we praise,
Who, robed in human flesh, appears,
To bless us in the end of days.
Dark hades saw the light arise,
And quick the darkness fled away;
The nations saw Thy waking beams,
When dawned the Resurrection day.

II

Glory, O Christ, to Thee we give,
The Head of our Salvation Thou;
For death is vanquished by Thy power,
And men are saved from wandering now.
The angel choirs in heaven rejoice,
For messengers of death are spurned;
The fall of Adam Thou hast raised,
And Satan's power is overturned.

III

We, all unworthy, stand around
Thy life inspiring grave, and raise
To Thy great tenderness of heart,
O Christ our Lord, a hymn of praise;
For thou gav'st welcome to the Cross,
Nor thrust the hand of death away,
That thou, O Lover of our race,
Mightst give the Resurrection day.

Rev. John Brownlie

IV

Word with the Father in the past,
Word with the Father aye to reign;
Mysterious born, to live and die,
And in His glory rise again.
O God of life to thee we sing,
Saviour of our souls, to Thee
Let hymns from every heart arise,
And everlasting glory be.

STICHERA OF THE ASCENSION
ho kurios anelephthe eis ouranous
Pentecostarion, p. 147

I

Now the Lord from earth ascending,
Seeks the throne of heaven again,
That the Comforter, descending,
Might abide with sinful men.

II

Clouds His chariots, upwards rising
Bear Him proudly to the skies;
Heaven beholds a sight surprising,
Man above the angels rise.

III

Lift your gates ye powers supernal;
All ye nations come adore;
For the Christ to realms eternal,
Goes to dwell forevermore.

Rev. John Brownlie

HYMN TO THE TRINITY

hos hai taxeis nun ton angelon en ourano
Horologion, p. 44

I

As angel hosts with heavenly songs,
Before Thy throne adore Thee,
So would we Lord, in humbler strains,
Pour out our hearts before Thee.

II

Forever blessed be Thy name,
Thrice Holy, we revere Thee;--
Shew mercy as Thy people now,
In fear and hope draw near Thee.

III

Thou from eternal ages, God,
The Heaven of heavens containing;
Thou Christ our Lord, Thou Spirit good,
In Trinity remaining.

IV

Daring like cherubim on high,
Who praising stand around Thee,
We bring the tribute of our hearts,
And with our praise surround Thee.

HYMN TO THE TRINITY
tas ano Dunameis mimoumenoi hoi epi ges
Horologion, p. 43

I

Our hearts to Heaven upraising,
We, with the angelic host,
Sing praises to the Father,
To Son, and Holy Ghost.

II

O Uncreated Nature,
Yet Maker Thou of all,
Our lips proclaim Thy praises,
As at Thy feet we fall.

III

All Holy, Holy, Holy,
Eternal God art Thou,--
Hear us in prayer before Thee,
And send Thy mercy now.

IV

In slumber Thou hast kept us,
And now, with morning light,
Our hearts and minds awaken,
And give them morn for night.

V

And we shall give Thee praises
Blest Trinity adored;
For Holy, Holy, Holy,
Art Thou Eternal Lord.

Rev. John Brownlie

HYMN TO THE TRINITY
humnodias ho kairos, kai deeseos hora
Horologion, p. 44

I

This is the time of song,
The hour when prayer is made,
And fervently we cry to Thee
O Undivided Trinity;--
Holy, Holy, Holy Thou,
God of Hosts to Whom we bow.

II

Even as the Heavenly hosts,--
But with unworthy lips,--
Eternal Trinity most strong,
To Thee we raise victorious song,
And falling down before Thee now,
Sing Holy, Holy, Holy Thou.

III

Thou Who wast born on earth,
But still with God remained,
Accept us Christ our God we pray,
As with angelic hosts we say,
Holy, Holy, Holy Thou,
With Thy mercy bless us now.

ORDER OF HOLY UNCTION
(From the Canon of Arsenius)
Ode III
su monos on thaumastos, kai en anthropois tois pistois hileos
Euchologion, p. 261

I

Thou Christ alone art great,
In Thee we ever find
Infinite love and tenderness,
And mercy wondrous kind.

II

Now in Thy love divine,
Come to the sufferers' aid;
In mercy Lord be merciful,
On Whom our wounds were laid.

III

Thy sanctifying grace,
O Christ send from above;
Seal Thou our souls and bodies now,
And heal us all in love.

Rev. John Brownlie

ORDER OF HOLY UNCTION
Kathisma
hos theios potamos, tou eleous huparchon
Euchologion, p. 261

I

A stream of mercy springs
O Christ our Lord from Thee;
Compassionate art Thou,
And full of sympathy.

II

Let now our eyes be turned,
To where that mercy flows;
Reveal Thy love divine,
And heal our smarting woes.

III

O may that wondrous stream
Flow plenteously apace;
That we may cleansed be,
We now entreat Thy grace.

FROM THE CANON OF THE DEAD
Ode VIII
statheros tous agonas epideixamenoi
Euchologion, p. 412

I

Who toiled for Christ through suffering sore,
And meekly grief and anguish bore;
And in their service steadfast strove,
To serve the Master Whom they love,--
Now rest in His eternal peace,
Through ages that shall never cease.

II

Who toil as they, and faithful prove
The servants of the Lord they love,
When toil is o'er and suffering past,
Enter the bliss of heaven at last,--
And rest in His eternal peace,
Through ages that shall never cease.

IDIOMELA OF S. JOHN THE MONK
poia tou biou truphe diamenei lupes ametochos;
Euchologion, p. 413

I

What joy of life abideth,
Without the smart of woe?
What glory lingers fadeless
Upon our world below?

II

All is a fleeting shadow,
And all a fitful gleam,
For death with cruel swiftness,
Dissolves the illusive dream.

III

O Christ a light unfailing,
A beauty lasting, rare,
Shines in Thy face to charm us,
And cheer us everywhere.

IV

Where Thou art aye abiding,
Where we that light may see,
Grant us, O Christ our Saviour,
For evermore to be.

STICHERON
(From the Burial Office for a Layman)
horontes me aphonon kai apnoun prokeimenon
Euchologion, p. 419

I

Come friends behold me here,
Speechless and breathless lying;
Held in the arms of death;--
Come with your tears and sighing.

II

But yesterday I lived,
And walked, and spoke with you:
Come friends, with the last kiss.
Bid me a long adieu.

III

For I shall walk no more
The wonted paths we trod;
My voice is stilled, I go
To speak alone with God.

IV

The Judge has called me hence,--
To Whom the wise and great,
The warrior and the king,
Are men of one estate.

V

Ah! not the name I bore
Shall final doom recall;
The life of each lies bare,
Before the Judge of all.

VI

For all the good I've done,
For all the ill and blame,--
Shall come to me in full,

Rev. John Brownlie

The honour or the shame.

VII
Call ye on Christ our God
That by His saving might,
I may a dwelling find
Among the sons of light.

STICHERA
(From the Burial Office for a Child)
o tis me threnesei teknon mou
Euchologion, p. 481

I

Who would not weep my child
To see thee still and dead?--
Thou from maternal arms,
Even as a bird hast fled:--
Who would not weep my child?

II

Who would not weep my child
To see thy faded brow,
Once like the lily, fair,
But lost to beauty now?--
Who would not weep my child?

III

Who would not weep my child?--
Like ship on boundless sea,
That leaves no track behind,
Lo, thou art gone from me,--
Who would not weep my child?

Rev. John Brownlie

STICHERA
paradeise pantime, to horaiotaton kallos
Triodion, p. 62

I

O Paradise above!
In glory all excelling;
There hath the God of love,
Fixed an eternal dwelling;
There loveliest beauty shines,
And pleasure endless thrills;
There love the soul entwines,
And peace the bosom fills.
The saints of God frequent its bowers,
And whispers fan its fragrant flowers.

II

Here would I humbly fall,
Before my God adoring,
That He may heed the call,
I bring to Him imploring;
And open wide the gate,
Closed by the hand of sin,
That, with the saints, thus late,
I yet may enter in;
And taste the tree of life that grows,
To heal the smart of mortal woes.

Centos and Suggestions

VAIN THE BLISS FROM EARTH THAT SPRINGS
(From the Burial Office for a Layman)
alethos mataiotes ta sumpanta
Euchologion, p. 409

I

Vain the bliss from earth that springs,--
Life is but an empty shade;
All our toil its bounty brings,
Made of what our dreams are made.

II

When with toil the mountain's height
Lies beneath our weary feet;
When the goal we kept in sight,
Yields the victory to the fleet;--

III

Fades the landscape from our view,
Droops the laurel on our brow,
False the things we thought were true,
Gone the joys that lured us, now.

IV

Ah! the world we gain to lose,
Ends our triumph with the grave;
All earth's wealth and power refuse
What vain hope exulting gave.

V

Christ, Thou Lover of our race,
When the strife of earth is o'er,
Give our weary souls a place,
In Thy Kingdom evermore.

Rev. John Brownlie

HAIL! THE MORN WITH GLADNESS CROWNED

I

Hail! the morn with gladness crowned,
Morn of morns, O glad and glorious!
When the Lord of Life, renowned,
Brake the bands of death, victorious.

II

Hades gazed in dread surprise,
As the light the darkness sundered;
Prisoners raised their weary eyes
Lit with hope, and mutely wondered.

III

Wounded was the Victor's brow,
Where the angry thorns distressed it;
But the conqueror's laurel now
Winding, on His forehead rested.

IV

Hail! the Man from death arisen.
Hail! the Christ a Victor glorious.
Thou hast broken hades' prison,
Christ, the Son of God, victorious.

CLOSE BESIDE THE HEART THAT LOVES ME

I

Close beside the heart that loves me
Would I rest in sorrow's hour,
With a Father's smile above me,
And beneath an arm of power.

II

Weak and worthless, worn and weary,
Welcome bids my faith be strong;
Sorrow's hour is short if dreary,
Joy shall last through ages long.

III

Dark the hour, but comes the morrow,
Dawn shall waken by and by;
Light shall gild the clouds of sorrow,
When the sun is in the sky.

IV

Rest, my soul, that love unfailing
Strengthens in the hour of woe,--
For the pain thy life assailing
Found Him when he dwelt below.

V

'Tis a heart that knows the sorrow,
Trust it when the night comes down;--
Tears shall yield to song to-morrow,
Night to morn, and cross to crown.

Rev. John Brownlie

THE TIME SHALL SURELY COME

I

The time shall surely come,
The hour is drawing near,
When in the clouds of heaven the Lord
To mortals shall appear.

II

Not in a lowly garb,
Shall we the Lord descry,
But decked in glory like the sun,
That lights the morning sky.

III

Not as in former days,
To pain and suffering sore,--
He comes to judge, Who came to save,--
To reign for evermore.

IV

Then, O my soul, awake!
Put on thy garb of light,
Look for the dawn that brings the day,
All glorious and bright.

V

Wait, for the hour is nigh;
Watch, for His coming nears;
Be thou the faithful servant then,
When He, thy Lord, appears.

THE TRANSFIGURATION

I

When glory crowned the mountain top,
And Christ was decked in garments fair,
The prophets of the Lord appeared,
And talked with the Redeemer there.

II

"Let us make this our dwelling-place,"
'Twas thus his followers made request;
"For it is good to linger here,
And they who dwell with Thee are blest."

III

Then from a cloud a voice was heard,
While each in terror held his breath,--
"This is My Own beloved Son,
Hear ye what the Belovéd saith."

IV

Jesus, when Thy glory gilds
The mount of God whereon we meet,
May we the voice from Heaven discern,
And bow expectant at Thy feet.

Rev. John Brownlie

BEYOND THE CLOUDS OF HEAVEN

I

Beyond the clouds of Heaven,
The Lord of life ascends;
Behold Him rise towards the skies,
Who for our race was given.

II

He came to earth Whose grace
Hath made our vileness clean;
That we may rise towards the skies,
And serve before His face.

III

He dwelt on earth Who gave
Himself for sinful man,--
That we may rise towards the skies,
Whom he came down to save.

IV

We would no longer gaze,
O Christ, to where Thou art,--
But, that we rise, towards the skies,
Do Thou Thy servants raise.

TRIPLE BEAM OF GLORY

I

Triple Beam of glory,
Through the darkness poured;
One the Light eternal
In our blessed Lord:
Give us in the morning,
Gladness for the day,--
All our life adorning,
Chase the night away.

II

Glory of the Father,
Glory of the Son,
Glory of the Spirit,
Blessed Three in One:
Let Thy beams united--
Brighter than the sun,
Lighten men benighted--
Blessed Three in One.

III

Men in darkness sitting
Scan the eastern skies,--
Glory of the Father,
On their night arise.
Give the morn supernal,
Give the endless day;--
Light of light eternal,
Banish night away.

IV

Hearts are dark with sorrow,
Minds are dull with care,
Clouds of doubt envelop
Mankind everywhere.
Triple Beam of gladness,
Through the ages poured,
Give us joy for sadness,--
Shine upon us, Lord.

O GOD OF LIGHT AND LIFE AND JOY

I

O God of Light and Life and Joy,
Blest Trinity! my soul employ
While I have power to sing:
No song too glad to raise to Thee,
Eternal, glorious Trinity,--
No gift too rich to bring.

II

When darkness brooded o'er the earth,
At thy command light had its birth,
And night and darkness fled;
And still, where hearts are bound in night,
Thou speak'st the word, "Let there be light,"
And noontide beams are shed.

III

Death held the Christ of God enchained,
The grave the Lord of Life restrained,
And eyes were filled with tears;--
Awoke the morn in eastern skies!
Behold, the Lord of Life arise!
Farewell to mortal fears!

IV

O joyless still the spirit sighs,
And fearful looks to ebon skies,
And stars begin to shine;--
Lo! overhead the bright array,
The night is shining as the day,
When hopes and fears entwine.

V

O God of Light and Life and Joy,
Blest Trinity, my soul employ
While I have power to sing:
No song too glad to raise to Thee,
Eternal, glorious Trinity,
No gift too rich to bring.

THE MORN IN BEAUTY BREAKS

I

The morn in beauty breaks,
The world to life awakes,
Up, soul of mine and sing;
And let the day begun,
In hours of service run,
And joy to duty bring.

II

The darkness fades away,
Light ushers in the day,--
Let there be light for me!
That round my path no cloud
Dark folding may enshroud,
Me in perplexity.

III

To Father and to Son,
To Spirit, Three in One,
Eternal praise be given:
Sung by the saints above,
In songs of fervent love,
Up in the choirs of heaven.

SEE WHERE THE ORB OF DAY

I

See where the orb of day
In glory sinks to rest,
The clouds of gold and purple crown
The mountains of the west;
And eve in silence brings
The night on dusky wings.

II

It is the hour of peace,
And hearts to heaven ascend,--
Come with your burdens and your care,
To an unchanging Friend;
And let the passing day,
Bear all your fears away.

III

It is the hour of prayer;
Let every fault be known;
Unveil the secrets of the soul,
And every sin disown;
The blood for sinners spilt,
Shall bear away your guilt.

IV

It is the hour of praise,
Let joy the stillness break;
And every grateful thought of God
To living song awake;
And saints in heaven shall bear
To God your fervent prayer.

Rev. John Brownlie

V

The night in silence falls,--
O God to Thee be praise!
And to the Spirit and the Son,
Throughout the endless days;--
Eternal Three in One,
While endless ages run.

www.ingramcontent.com/pod-product-compliance
Lightning Source LLC
Chambersburg PA
CBHW032011080426
42735CB00007B/573